IN SEARCH OF WORDS

FOOTNOTES VISUAL THINKING TECHNIQUES

OLIVER P.B. WEST

Published in 2008 by Oliver P.B. West

oliver@oliverwest.net

ISBN 978-0-9560910-0-0

Compiled & edited by Jeremy Barham from transcriptions by Elizabeth A. West and dictations by Oliver P.B. West.

Names used in Case Studies have been changed, except Alice Povey's.

This book is dedicated to all those children who can't sit still in class.

CONTENTS

EDITOR'S NOTE

Western society is dominated by words. Linear, lexical information transmission is the norm, and most of us don't think twice about it. We train our children to think and learn in words from a very early age, marginalising alternative ways of processing information. We know that children learn through play, but we hope that they learn to read and write sooner rather than later. We assume that traditional words-based teaching and training methods are right and proper, and that people who don't get on with them lack a degree of intelligence. Every now and then a successful entrepreneur mentions that he or she is dyslexic, and we look at their extraordinary success and secretly wonder how on earth they managed to pull it off, especially with such a poor education.

This prejudice is unacceptable. Our schools are squeezing non-linear thinkers out to the margins, quashing creativity and variety in a bid to produce pupils who will pass national exams. Many of these marginalised learners are branded with a 'learning difficulty' label, when often their difficulty lies with the teaching methods they are subjected to rather than their intellects.

Oliver West is on a mission to bring alternative teaching methods to the classroom and lecture hall. I have watched people cry at his talks as for the first time somebody at the front validates their way of thinking, affirms their intelligence and celebrates their differences. I have watched teachers finally understanding what might be going through the heads of those disruptive learners in their classrooms who seem intelligent, but just can't get anything done.

This book has been pieced together partly by dictation, but mainly from transcriptions of Oliver's talks faithfully typed by his mother over the last ten years. I hope you enjoy it.

Jeremy Barham

PREFACE

My experience in school was very painful. I was eventually labelled as chronically dyslexic, and I recall embarrassment after embarrassment as I struggled to cope with the classroom environment. From coming out with the wrong words and being clumsy, to forgetfulness and daydreaming – all served to make me feel extremely uncomfortable throughout my childhood. I went to seven different schools, none of which knew what to do with me, and pretty soon any confidence I started out with had been quashed. I started to believe the message that had been sent back to my parents, that I wouldn't actually get any qualifications, and that all I would be able to do would be something fairly menial.

And so for the last twelve years or so I have been trying to figure out how and why they got it wrong, and also how and why it has taken me so long to break out of the pronouncement that was placed upon me. In fact it's still a daily battle, and if you talk to any dyslexic you'll find that that uncomfortable feeling is there as powerfully as when they were a child. They might now have strategies to deal with it, but it's just as much at the forefront of their minds. Whenever I talk to dyslexics and we start sharing similar experiences, their emotion is right there, always on the surface. They don't talk about the past, they're talking about last week, about today.

This book is for those people, and for others who want to better understand or teach them. It is also for those who may not be dyslexic but who would benefit from learning in a more visual way.

In the first half of the book I describe the characteristics of visual thinkers and those with dyslexic tendencies, and the text is presented in a more traditional font and line spacing. The second half of the book is an introduction to my Footnotes visual thinking techniques, and for this section the text has been presented in a more 'dyslexia-friendly' format (grey text to reduce contrast, larger font size, increased line spacing) for two reasons: firstly to make that part of the book more accessible to dyslexic readers, and secondly to contrast with the first half and thereby give the 'linear' reader a graphic example of the visual preferences of a dyslexic reader. In the right hand margin of this section, Alice Povey has drawn examples of Footnotes images alongside the text, just as they would be used to annotate a piece of writing. Her images might not mean anything to you – the idea is simply to show how a reader might use Footnotes. Alice is a dyslexic illustrator who learnt Footnotes techniques while at University College Falmouth, and you can read more about her in the illustrated case study on page 42. There is also a lot of white space around the text throughout the whole book – please use this space to make notes in words or pictures.

INTRODUCTION

I now realise that not being helped at any stage in my education forced me to come up with my own personalised ways of coping. These painful years were the foundation for 'Footnotes', my visual thinking techniques for learning and personal development. After struggling through a Fine Art degree I started working in primary schools as an artist, and quickly found that I was connecting with children that teachers had practically given up on. I started getting phone calls from teachers saying things like, "What did you do?! You did something that day that I can't put my finger on…" and "The children you spent time with are behaving differently now – they are able to concentrate better. How did you do that?" They wanted to know what I had said or done in one day, or sometimes just one conversation, that had brought about some quite dramatic changes in certain children.

My first answers were "I don't know!", and I had to go away and think about what it was that I was doing to help. I eventually realised that I was understanding and connecting with children who, like me, did not think in linear terms. When I came into contact with a child who was 'talking all over the place' instead of putting one word in front of the next, I was able to track with them. I was able to understand the children who confused everyone else because I was talking and listening in visual terms, talking about what they could see in their minds but had not managed to communicate in a linear way. My understanding did not come from research or theory, I simply recognised their way of thinking as being like mine.

I began to apply my own learning strategies with the children I met in schools, and soon developed a collection of techniques and ideas for helping visual thinkers and those with dyslexic tendencies. My understanding of how visual thinkers and dyslexics think and learn has since grown significantly as I have met more and more children and adults with unique ways of seeing the world. In this book I will share some of my ideas, and my dream would be that our educational systems are transformed by a new understanding of visual thinking and dyslexia.

CHARACTERISTICS OF DYSLEXICS AND VISUAL THINKERS

Learners who think in a non-linear way are very often sidelined in a normal classroom. They can be distracting to other learners, so they are given ancillary support which can unfortunately draw them away from the teacher. This need not happen to such an extent if teachers are given the tools to offer visual learning strategies to visual learners within the normal classroom environment.

Money is being poured into universities and schools for dyslexics, for laptops, spelling aids etc., but those who have dyslexic tendencies that 'aren't bad enough' are losing out. Visual learners will fall into this category, and something needs to change to help them. Many so-called dyslexics are strongly visual thinkers – if their learning needs were met there would be less need for dyslexia solutions. The emergence of the 'Individual Learning Plan' in U.K. schools is a positive step towards discovering the preferred learning method of each individual; incorporating each learning style within the classroom is the next stage.

When they arrive at university a lot of students find that they can't write an essay. In school they have often been given factual information in a logical, step-by-step, linear order, and they learn to reproduce that information in an essay. They may well have become experts in this linear way of thinking. However, at university they need to present arguments, have opinions and approach a subject from various angles; this requires a holistic perspective as well as a step-by-step one. This more personal perspective is a struggle for most students, who are used to a right or wrong answer, so the ones who are usually good at reading and writing and have never found essays hard are surprised to find that even they can't write this kind of essay. This is when using pictures to contain a holistic perspective and work out how to structure an essay becomes very useful. However, many students who have not exercised this technique, having probably not needed to use it at school, find that it takes time to 'wake up' the visual part of the brain. A better balance of thinking techniques in school would really help here; learners need to be adaptable, to be able to think and process information in different ways. Encouraging learners at an early age to experiment with visual thinking techniques that they are not as familiar or confident with may well set them up to be more adaptable later in their lives. Dyslexics often benefit more noticeably than others from using visual thinking strategies. Indeed they often learn such strategies inherently.

A high percentage of Art and Design students have dyslexic issues; they have already found that they are comfortable with visual thinking and have gravitated towards this discipline. They need to express themselves in ways that are not necessarily logically understood, and of course 'art' gives the wide remit that they need to do that. On the other hand, students who are well versed in linear thinking and are used to delivering assessment requirements in linear terms need to be encouraged to break out of those prescribed restrictions and find the freedom to express themselves in a non-linear manner. They very often need to be given permission to do this, because for their entire school career it has not been an option. Quite often this leads to students not writing an essay at all, but presenting their work in an entirely different way. The rapid visual presentation of vast quantities of information is normal outside the academic world, from animated websites to fast-moving television documentaries with images that flash up for a split second. This kind of creative expression needs to be encouraged in education – we need to break out of the idea that thinking in linear terms is the best way of thinking. In order to accommodate visual learners in our educational systems, we must first properly understand how they think and how they can be encouraged to release their true potential.

Many visual thinkers in classrooms today feel disabled, and are treated as such. I long for visual thinkers to realise that they have an ability that others don't have, and to realise that they see and experience the world in an incredible way. My hope is that all of us can better understand and appreciate the different ways that people learn.

The following pages describe some of the most common traits of visual thinkers and those with dyslexic tendencies. This is a very personal subject for me, so you will find me describing myself in much of what follows.

Processing

1. Picture thinking

I am a visual thinker first and foremost and pictures are my first language – English is my second. It has been very helpful for me to accept that I am allowed to think in my first language, even though I then need to communicate in English because I live in the U.K. I find it easy to connect with international students whose first language is not English, as we struggle with similar issues. I regularly work in international school classrooms where there are as many mother tongues as there are learners! In this context, picture thinking removes language barriers very effectively.

I can't think clearly without seeing a picture. If I can't mentally visualise a picture from the words that are being communicated to me, I will rarely understand those words properly. This is often very embarrassing if I am asked a direct and simple question. I used to feel very thick at school because the questions were simple, yet I struggled to verbalise a response; what made this worse were the responses of the teachers, who would repeat the questions more slowly, which of course made no difference and only served to humiliate me further. When the teacher asked a question to the class I would put my hand up because I knew the answer, but somehow the answers I gave were not the ones the teacher was looking for; somebody else would then put their hand up and give the 'correct' answer that in my mind was the same as mine but verbalised in a different way. Their answer would match the picture in my mind, but not the words that I had said – my words came out the wrong way round.

Dyslexics will often start interrupting as soon as somebody else has started answering because they want to say, "I knew that!" But if you then return to that person and give them the opportunity to answer it's usually gone by then. In a split second their mind has moved on. Dyslexics will get quieter and quieter in the classroom because of this issue.

I have heard dyslexia specialists say, "Whatever you do, don't confuse them. Say the same words again and again. Don't confuse them with new ones, just keep on repeating it." This is rarely effective for a visual thinker. If I didn't manage to picture in my mind what was being said the first time, I won't get it the next because I haven't been able to form a picture with those particular words - it doesn't matter how slowly the words are spoken or how many times they are repeated. Repeating something in the hopes that eventually the listener will understand will exacerbate feelings of frustration in both learner and teacher. It is much more effective to rephrase the sentence and, ironically, add in *more* information. This gives the visual thinker a broader context, and by filling in missing information helps him or her to create a mental picture. Visual thinkers need the ins and outs and whys – not because they need to be in control (a common misconception), but because they need to be able to frame what is being communicated within a bigger picture.

One word can make all the difference between a dyslexic understanding what a teacher wants or not. When instructing a visual thinker, it is helpful to try and make sure that the sentence contains words that are pictorial. Being aware that the listener will be receiving the information in visual terms can help to think about what particular word will stimulate a picture, and then what sentence can be constructed around it. This may sound time-consuming, but comes easily with practice; to be able to communicate like this to visual

thinkers would solve one of the main communication issues found in the classroom, and in many other social environments as well.

I find that for dyslexics one carefully picked word is often a better trigger for a thought process than a whole sentence. The whole sentence can detract from the point, but one word can prompt a picture that 'says a thousand words'. Careful choice of imagery is therefore very important for visual thinkers. I will talk later about one of my early reading strategies where I remove all images from words in reading books. If the image is supplied in the book, the child must try and learn the word and the associated image, storing this information in the memory. However, if they have to create their own images for each word, they create a personal, imaginative pathway in a different part of the brain. Instead of trying to purely memorise, they are having to process the word they read and create a unique picture association with it. In this way they learn to decode language using their own visual imaginations.

2. Holistic thinking

Dyslexics are often hard to teach in a traditional way, because they aren't very good at following the teacher's step-by-step thoughts and information sequences. I often talk about shepherding dyslexics, and acting like a mirror for them to understand their own thinking processes. It is so important that they are aware of the process they're going through to arrive at an understanding of something. They can't just be told how, they have to experience how – they have to *discover*. Information can't just be given and expected to stay – they have to go through a process of making it real for themselves so that they can access it later.

This is frustrating for those working with or leading people like this, as learners need to take control and do it themselves to be able to learn aspects of the subject. This is another reason why areas of education that are encouraging the Individual Learning Plan have seen great improvement for individuals such as dyslexics: they are able to develop student enquiry-based learning strategies, developing their own projects and developing ways of presenting their findings in such a way that they can show evidence of the things that they have learnt and truly do know.

For this to happen, the teachers have to exercise great restraint and trust, and often patience, while the individuals get used to not being led but leading themselves. Given the opportunity and encouragement to do this, the individuals will soon develop methods for effective motivation and achievement of targets within a certain time. Dyslexics commonly find these requirements difficult without discovering strategies that help them learn. Once this has been achieved, their skills are noticeably heightened and they often leave many of the other issues in their learning environment way behind, even in their use of language, as they find ways of translating thoughts from one 'language' to another. This is why I find it useful to think of their picture language as their first language, bearing in mind that they will have to translate from this language if they want a broader section of their community to understand and communicate with them.

I find it very difficult to follow someone else's instructions, and very simple instructions are much harder to follow than complicated ones. A complicated question with lots of facets and viewpoints is something I can look at holistically and piece together. A simple, direct question is much harder, because it often doesn't have a wider context in which I can frame it. A simple question that might seem to have one answer for a linear thinker can be perceived as being non-precise by a visual thinker. Teachers are often baffled by visual thinkers who appear to be over-complicating simple questions in an attempt to understand them!

I find it very difficult to bring all the thoughts in my head into one small sentence, another reason why easy questions are harder for me to answer than hard ones. At school I was in the bottom stream – the E stream, but I found it easier to do the C stream homework. Simplifying the questions took away the context that was vital to my understanding. I had only the bare bones, but I needed the flesh – I needed to see how all the information fitted together and why. But this information is often left out to 'simplify' what is being taught, or quite simply because there isn't time in the lesson to pad out the basics.

In very general terms, the left side of the brain deals with the ordering and sequencing of information, while the right side deals with the emotional and creative side of things. Someone who has a dominant left side has the ability to filter stimuli entering the brain from the various senses, allowing them to focus clearly on one thing or thought whilst ignoring the other input. I, on the other hand, have a strongly dominant right side of the brain, so I deal with all the stimuli at once – there is very little automatic sequencing of input. I am literally thinking and processing many things at the same time. While this may sound like a nightmare to a linear thinker, I actually need a variety of stimuli at the same time in order to concentrate, so I find that I fidget – physical movement helps me to focus and to process information. I may move a pencil and doodle, or move my hands or legs.

I find it hard to sit still for any length of time, and prefer to move around when I am listening to someone. It is very difficult for me to focus intently and directly on one specific stimulus. The physical movement can sometimes be quite impulsive, and I often won't realise I am moving.

Dyslexic children in a classroom will sometimes subconsciously process information visually and act upon it without realising they have done so, spontaneously leaping out of their chairs to run across the classroom and give someone a ruler because they have noticed he doesn't have one; their strong sense of justice and fairness means that they feel the need to immediately redress the imbalance that they have visually picked up on. Dyslexics and visual thinkers often have a deep awareness of justice because their brains makes long-reaching connections. In this example the child sees that a classmate lacks a ruler, thinks of the implications of this and wants to rectify the situation.

As a landscape artist and printmaker, holistic thinking is essential for my creative process, which is often multi-layered and quite the opposite of a linear, logical expression.

Sequencing

I find it very hard to deal with sequencing in any context. I panic if I start thinking about what I'm going to say next, for instance. Having a list, or notes, that were planned on a prior occasion, and then having to remember why I put the contents in that order, is very difficult for me. I find it much better to work with what I've got in my mind at the time. I use words and ideas a bit like an artist uses a palette – I have the information in my head (and sometimes down on paper in picture form), but there is no list telling me what I have to do or what order I have to do it in. If I see an image and it doesn't remind me of anything, that's OK. It's the pressure of seeing things in an order that doesn't work for me. As long as I am free to choose the sequence on the spot, at the time I need it, then I am OK.

One of the side-effects of the sequencing issue is poor short-term memory. Information that is given to me in linear form, in written or spoken words, is extremely difficult for me to process. When the next word arrives, my mind moves onto it and leaves the last word behind. This can make me look a bit stupid when I am unable to listen to simple step-by-step instructions and remember them. But actually what I need is all the instructions at once, so a diagram is ideal. I need to be able to visualise the input in order to remember it.

Speaking

Ten years ago, at the age of 26, I struggled to speak in clear sentences. I have learned since then to string a sentence together in a linear manner, using my own visual thinking techniques. As visual thinking techniques are developed, sentence structure tends to improve.

"Slow down, I've lost you!" and, "One step at a time!" are phrases I hear all the time. I sometimes try to communicate all the parallel thoughts in my head at the same time, and in no particular order! I am often not fully aware of all the thoughts I am having, and therefore find it hard to hold my thoughts together, sequence them, and then communicate them. Consequently I can come across as rather confused, with my thoughts coming out randomly and in broken sentences. If I can clearly see all my thoughts, I am more able to choose the order I want to communicate them in. This is when a visual memory prompt which is outside my mind can help me visualise my thoughts and then consider which ones I want to be led by. We will see later on how I use the Footnotes Grid in this way.

When I speak publicly at seminars and conferences I have learnt to progress through my topic using picture thinking, but my sentences can still be in bits and pieces and I constantly go off at tangents. Visual thinkers are often paranoid that they are coming across as rambling wafflers, but they usually speak with passion and depth as they find it not worth the effort otherwise! In fact if I'm not passionate about something that I'm trying to talk about, I will struggle to communicate it clearly. If I am not interested in what I'm saying, it's as if I can't access the intellect to be able to talk about it. Passion enables me to 'hyper-focus' (see later section), and in that state I am able to speak much more clearly.

I sometimes start or finish my sentences halfway through, and think I have said a whole sentence. I have imagined, or pictured the sentence in my mind, and the verbal communication of that sentence can follow haphazardly.

Often a portion of the sentence is lost in the transition (or translation) from mind to mouth, but I have no realisation of this. I find it hard to say the obvious words and sometimes don't notice that I've not said them because I'm so focused on the real crux of the point I want to make. My mind completes the rest of the sentence, while sometimes only one word actually comes out of my mouth! I have often found that people say to me, "You didn't say that!" when I am convinced that I did.

Linear thinkers can therefore find it very difficult to track with me and follow what I'm saying, but I have a bizarre connection with other visual thinkers, who can flit from subject to subject following my train of picture thought.

Distraction…

Being a 'holistic' thinker, I can cope with all sorts of thoughts going on at the same time, on many levels. One advantage of this is that in a moving and changing environment, holistic thinking gives much more adaptability and gives the ability to make a fast assessment of available information having quickly looked at all the alternatives. Consequently many dyslexics come across as being particularly sure and confident in certain situations because it's clear to them what all the options are, and they can then make choices more quickly and easily. On the other hand, a big disadvantage of this holistic thinking is the consequent susceptibility to distraction. If I'm sitting in a pub, I am aware of other people's conversations. My brain subconsciously creates images from their words that pop into my conscious mind, and I find it difficult to tell whether those pictures are from my conversation or another one. I will even find myself answering questions from someone else's conversation, much to the confusion of my listener!

I therefore find this environment very uncomfortable – I'd much rather be outside where other sounds disperse more easily.

One of the external stimuli I am particularly sensitive to is other people's emotions. I have a heightened awareness of how people are feeling, and it often distracts me and can be overwhelming.

The susceptibility to distraction can be a real disadvantage for visual thinkers in a classroom situation, where learners are required to focus on one specific piece of information or input, sitting still with pens down and eyes focused; this is very, very difficult because they don't know what to do with all the other stuff going on in their heads. This is one reason why it is so important where a dyslexic sits in a classroom – what there is around him that will distract him. One day the light, movement and sound conditions might be conducive to more focused concentration, but on another day a particular stimulus could be constantly triggering a distraction response. Other children, noise from outside or another classroom, or even the air conditioning fan can all make it very hard for a dyslexic learner to concentrate on one thing.

There is one tendency that visual thinkers use to try and compensate which may make them appear very disruptive in the classroom – they may try and make noise in order to block out other noise that's stopping them from hearing the teacher. The unwanted noise is creating a stimulus in their minds that they don't want, so they make a noise to block out the distracting noise. This can be in the form of shouting at the teacher or murmuring, and worse still, they might not even be aware that they're doing it!

…and Hyper-focus

The opposite side of the distraction coin is the visual thinker's ability to be 'hyper-focused'. Once all distractions have been shut out, a dyslexic has the ability to be extremely highly focused on something or someone. In this state, they can achieve a lot, very quickly, as long as new distractions do not break their focus. This trait is one of the visual thinker's most useful assets – it is therefore vital that they are given the opportunity to get in this 'state'.

It is important for teachers to be aware of this trait, and to facilitate a learning environment where the dyslexic learner is not interrupted with breaks or subject changes, but allowed to engage in depth with what is being learnt. Giving little chunks of information and bitty tasks is actually not helpful.

I get frustrated when I go into a classroom and the teacher says "You won't get their concentration for more than twenty minutes, and then they'll need a break. Otherwise there will be a riot." If visual learners are only ever given twenty minute bite-sized chunks of teaching and then removed from that environment and placed in another, they will get used to being distracted. They will never really learn how to hyper-focus.

CASE STUDY: BILL

As a chef in a restaurant, Bill had to focus on different elements of the meal he had to produce. He had to decide what time he should start cooking each dish to match up with others from that table. The orders would come very close together, and Bill became very focused. But within a short period there would be a lull in the orders – this was hard for Bill as a dyslexic because he found it difficult to maintain concentration unless he stayed in his hyper-focused state (remembering that most dyslexics are one extreme or other – really, really concentrating or not concentrating at all). He had to be alert to hear instructions that were only given once, and from a number of sources. Sometimes they could come after there had been a lull in his cooking activity, so he was forever having to go from a hyper-focused state to having nothing to do, which meant he lost his concentration.

Someone shouted an new instruction, but it took a lot of energy for him to get hyper-focused again so he struggled to re-engage. When he came out of the hyper-focused state, he then became aware that he was tired or cold or hungry – all the other inputs that he had been blocking out arrived at that time. He had to push these away to get focused again because it was too exhausting to move in and out of hyper-focus too much.

His solution was to stay hyper-focused throughout the shift by creating other things to do in order to stay alert and focused. In other words juggling lots of things at the same time was better for him than short bursts of activity. The head chef had been giving him simpler and simpler things to do, which meant he was getting his work done quickly and then twiddling his thumbs. But rather than being 'kept back' and not given too much responsibility he was actually far more comfortable being given MORE responsibility.

Reading

I will often read a sentence, or even a whole story, and not properly comprehend it. As I read I create images of the words, but my short term memory is so bad that at the end of the story I have retained very little. I have so many images going through my mind and I haven't learnt a way to see all of them at once, so as the next image arrives it replaces the previous one. Because the current image is constantly changing and I don't have the ability to go back to the picture before, the older images are lost. If I could see them all, and could move on and keep the other images present, my comprehension would be far better.

I find it much easier to read 'untidy' hand-written text rather than a uniform font. Irregular writing requires a visual response – it is more of a picture than a code and therefore elicits a different processing response from my brain. I have therefore created my own 'untidy' font (used on the book cover and title page) which is a representation of my handwriting and can be downloaded into a word-processing program; I have also worked with eight students at Plymouth University on font creation for dyslexics.

Some dyslexics actually love reading certain types of writing because they discover the ability to master something they found difficult before. They also create a vocabulary of ideas that they then want to use to stimulate their imaginations. A lot of dyslexics love poetry because it gets to the

19

point quickly, not necessarily making sense, but often creating a picture very effectively.

My perception is that nowadays the predominant tools used in schools to aid spelling and reading skills are 'phonics' strategies. These involve sounding out letters, which has never really been effective for me. I am so visually dominant that 'sounds' just tend to confuse me. Quite a lot of learners will have a visual dominance, and then next would be kinaesthetic, followed by auditory. These learners are likely to find it difficult to focus on sounds because they are trying to make a connection with something movement based or physically experienced, rather than a sound that they can't store or hold for long. Because this audio memory is weak in comparison to their more dominant senses, they are unlikely to find phonics helpful to start with, although they can be effective when added to established visual thinking techniques.

Professor John Stein of Oxford University has been researching the physiological reasons for dyslexic reading behaviour. The following is quoted from a seminar he gave ("Visual Dyslexia: Force of Artistic Talent") at the 2003 Arts & Visual Thinking Conference in Falmouth:

"Reading requires precise sequencing of letters and word sounds, and in fact there is no other normal activity of human beings that requires such precise linear sequencing. But dyslexics are bad at this kind of sequencing… because they inherit a vulnerability of a particular kind of nerve cell in the brain called a Magna cell… Magna cells play a very important part in reading in particular, because they control how the eyes move during reading. How the eyes move during reading determines how you sequence things – how you sequence small objects such as letters."

He has found that due to a developmental deficiency in Magna cell formation in the brain, the eyes of dyslexics do not move from left to right in tiny movements like a 'normal' reader's eyes. They tend to make larger eye movements, and consequently find it very difficult to sequence letters and words. There are several ways to improve reading ability; I have found that dyslexics find it easier to read in columns – when working with children I limit the number of words to five per line. Coloured lenses have proven to be very effective for some dyslexics, and Professor Stein has shown that this is because Magna cells are particularly sensitive to yellow and blue light, and so by wearing coloured lenses the Magna cellular system can be boosted to improve reading.

During the 2003 conference Professor Stein went on to say:

"I want to emphasise that I'm not talking about seeing big objects, seeing pictures, seeing the whole landscape, that's a different kind of visual processing. Because quite often people assume that if you are bad at one kind of visual processing that you will be bad at all kinds of visual processing, and that is not true….If you are bad at this fine linear sequencing required for reading, it is often the case that you are particularly good at large, holistic, visual, spatial kinds of processing."

In fact, although dyslexics find it hard to move their eyes in tiny jumps from letter to letter and word to word, they have a natural ability to 'speed read' through a larger amount of text, taking in the overall content of a piece of writing. Because they process in a more holistic way rather than linearly, they can make connections within large amounts of information.

Dyslexics are said to be keen-sighted, and will often be the children in a group that will notice the smallest details of change in their environment. As adults, many dyslexics excel in the arts and in other careers where visual-spatial awareness is important. Many architects have dyslexic tendencies, and their ability to see a three-dimensional design before it is drawn is extremely beneficial. Many highly successful entrepreneurs are dyslexic, having the ability to see the bigger picture; rather than focusing too much on one aspect of a business, they are able to see all areas at the same time, using their creativity and visual imagination to see possibilities that others may have missed.

Writing

When I was in school I remember finding it harder to learn to hold the pencil correctly than the children around me, and was always being told to not push so hard. As a child I would regularly indent a page of handwriting into many layers of paper in my efforts to try and coordinate the pencil better because it felt as though it was going to go off course all the time.

When I had to do handwriting exercises, which seemed to happen forever because I was always being asked to repeat written work until the teacher could read what I'd written, the sensation when trying to control the pencil became so intense that I felt all the muscles in my neck tense up, right up through my back into the top of my head. At this point I would find that the strength would go from my right arm, and I would find it very hard to continue to hold the pencil so tightly. Without holding tightly, my handwriting became very erratic and would sometimes span three lines rather than one. This made handwriting tasks incredibly tiring, frustrating and humiliating.

I was often angry with myself, and sometimes with others if they showed little understanding of what I was experiencing. If only I had had the means as a child, and the understanding, to explain to them. Incidentally, my handwriting now is very similar to my writing when I was about 6 yrs old - I still press too hard!

When I am encouraging children who are being asked to produce hand-written work, I encourage them to loosen their grip on the pencil. Sometimes it's good to have a ruler to stop the handwriting going too far down into another line. The presence of the ruler being controlled by the other hand seems to encourage spatial awareness and control of both hands, maybe because if the other hand has something to do, then the body is somewhat more balanced, working on two things at once with both hands. Perhaps if children weren't forced to choose a writing hand they might find a better balance of brain activity (between left and right hemispheres) and consequently have more controlled and fluent writing if given a choice of which hand to use.

mate! you look shattered! how far have you run?!
no running... ...just writing!

Drawing

I used to get told by my biology teachers that my diagrams of dissected animals looked as though the animals were just about to walk off the page, when in fact all they wanted was tidy linear drawing with written labels marked with a ruler. The poor animals still looked as though they were alive! As I found it almost impossible to draw with lines, I would resort to shading the general shape of the body. Within art studies this showed up as an issue for a number of teachers who commented that I should try and draw more tidily - I got used to being told that a spider must have just run across my page.

My art skills were not particularly identified by anyone until in my mid-teens when I discovered oil painting and the ability to go over marks that I'd previously made. At this point, because I wasn't reliant on line, I had the ability to bring structure through tone and colour contrasts. Since then I have developed as an artist, very much reliant on tonal perspective rather than linear perspective in my work. (The physical reason for this may be to do with my eye movement – see the summary of research carried out by Professor John Stein on page 20 – in addition to dyspraxic tendencies that I have.) So despite much ridicule, I can be very co-ordinated as a scribbler! And I love encouraging those who say they can't draw to discover (possibly through their own dyspraxic tendencies) the ability to control their pencil, not through precision but through repetitive mark making. I believe this is one of many stimulants for the development of Footnotes strategies.

Listening

As a child I was told that I had selective hearing because although I could often repeat a question somebody had asked me back to them, I did not respond in any way. I now understand that often spoken words that don't stimulate images in my mind are not processed, even when my audio memory, from a short-term memory point of view, can recall word for word what I just heard. I believe that when trying to understand visual thinkers, it is important to be mindful of the link between audio and visual memory.

Visual thinkers are also prone to interrupting, and perhaps trying to finish sentences for people. This is sometimes interpreted as some sort of cockiness, and consequently here's another phrase a visual thinker is familiar with: "Let me finish – don't try and be clever and finish what I'm saying!", or "Why are you questioning what I'm saying – just listen!". The real reason for interrupting is quite the opposite of cockiness; visual thinkers often have an insecurity that they will get the wrong end of the stick. When interrupting they are simply needing to clarify that they've got the right picture in their minds of what the speaker is trying to communicate. Visual thinkers have vivid imaginations, and need to be quite sure that they are understanding what's being said and creating the right picture in their minds before letting their imaginations go. They are capable of rapid and highly creative thought, often visualising information and ideas much quicker than a linear thinker. But it can be humiliating to realise too late that your thoughts have been running off in the wrong direction.

Footnotes Techniques

Learners who think in a non-linear way are very often sidelined in a normal classroom. They can be distracting to other learners, so they are given ancillary support which can unfortunately draw them away from the teacher. The emergence of the 'Individual Learning Plan' in European schools is a positive step towards discovering the preferred learning method of each individual, but it can be daunting and exhausting for teachers to aim at incorporating many different teaching styles in the classroom all at the same time.

Teachers need to be given simple tools to offer visual learning strategies to learners within the normal classroom environment. Footnotes is a series of visual thinking and learning techniques that are straightforward to teach and easy to use. In this section of the book I will share some of the Footnotes techniques that have proven to be successful in many schools and universities across the U.K. and in Europe.

Most of the issues with writing stem from having to write sentences in which the writer must sequence letters, words and information. The pressure of having to sequence in this way can make a dyslexic or visual thinker freeze, and can stop them from saying or writing anything at all.

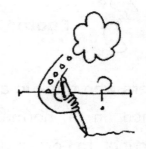

A picture, on the other hand, can holistically symbolise a piece of information without needing any sequencing at all. Unlike spelling or writing sentences, there is no right or wrong picture, so there is no pressure to get it right. Each person could draw something completely unique to symbolise their thoughts; the drawings could of course be translated into a linear form later, and could be written or described using different words each time if necessary. Without the pressure to produce correct sequencing, visual thinkers are far more free to express themselves and are much more likely to get out what's in their heads!

The use of drawn images to communicate underpins many Footnotes visual thinking techniques. The strategies are therefore not dependent on age or language because anyone can make images. The images do not have to mean anything for anyone else, so no drawing skill is required. If you are a teacher you might initially find it hard if you don't understand the image that has been drawn to remind the learner of a word or idea. But the freedom it affords a visual thinker, and the resulting creativity and expression, make the effort worthwhile.

Given the opportunity, a visual thinker could design a unique language of squiggles that nobody else understands, made up at his own pace and with his own logic. A vocabulary can be quickly built up, and the learner may well become fluent in their own language, feeling more comfortable with it than with their mother tongue. This gives the visual thinker a natural means of getting thoughts onto paper. The jump for a dyslexic from thoughts to words is a huge one, but from thoughts to pictures is a natural one. Translating drawn pictures to written words is of

course still a hurdle, but it's far more easily achievable.

I teach a lot of University students who have to write long essays. Holistic, visual thinkers will sit down at the computer to write an essay, and they might get out a few sentences before they stop because it doesn't sound right, or they haven't used the correct English, or the spelling needs correcting. But by the time they've gone back over those sentences to try and get them right they have lost about five other thoughts that they had when they were initially inspired to write. This is not only unproductive but extremely demoralising. The Footnotes answer is to **think and plan in holistic, pictorial terms, and then translate into linear terms**. Use pictures to 'say' what you want to say, and then translate them later. We will see later exactly how to do that.

I regularly work with students helping them to plan 8,000 word dissertations without requiring any written work at all other than a synopsis. One picture might represent 30 words, or even 3000. It won't be readable, but the student knows what it's all about. An analogy I use is of a memorable day, say somebody's wedding or birthday. When you look at photos of the event, you don't just remember the picture, you recall other things that happened at the event, even though those things are not in the photo. The images are not meant to encapsulate all the information – they are merely the trigger. I have had students with entire 20,000 word dissertations completely planned in pictures.

For some students, particularly artists, words are an inadequate medium for thoughts – they just don't 'say' what needs to be said. More and more schools and universities are accepting other forms of work for assessment, but this will always be a challenge. In most cases, however, a translation of some sort is possible, and in fact I wouldn't want to steal from a student the sense of achievement they get from actually handing in a great wadge of paper. For some people this is a huge wall they think they can never climb, so my aim with Footnotes is more to alleviate

the fear of written assignments, rather than do away with them.

I often get asked, "What if we allow learners to be so picture-based and image reliant that it actually affects their language and other linear skills that have to be demonstrated in examination-based work? If we are encouraging picture-based activities might we be leading them away from spending time developing their literary skills?" Fortunately quite the opposite seems to happen. What we are teaching them is to use their preferred style of thinking and processing information *internally*. By allowing these learners to communicate *with themselves* more effectively, they then find it easier to communicate externally by speaking or writing. Ten years ago I struggled to put words in the right order to make a sentence; by using my visual thinking strategies I can now think more clearly by creating images of what I want to say or write, and this has made my external communication much better. The more efficient use of the right side of my brain seems to service the left side more effectively.

You may be thinking that the drawing process I am describing sounds laborious and time-consuming. However, the relief it brings for visual thinkers, and the release of creativity that ensues, more than outweigh the investment of time and effort. Not only that, but new neural pathways are established that become more and more functional with time. For some children, these pathways are already established, but are just not exercised in traditional school environments that try to force a learner to think and process in a linear, lexical way. Just like a muscle, visual thinking can be exercised to make it work better; children that have found it difficult to focus and concentrate in lessons can suddenly find they are able to focus when they discover their preferred, natural thinking style and begin to regularly use it.

For others it takes practice, and to start with it can be a difficult thing to learn. But the more the brain is used in a certain way, the better it performs, and before long what was once a struggle becomes a natural process. It is common for there to be a

watershed time when it suddenly becomes natural – it 'pings'. I have heard from students up to two years later saying they've just 'pinged'.

Eventually, with practice, there is often no longer a need to actually draw images on paper; the mind gets used to connecting input with images and an internal whiteboard takes over from the piece of paper.

Many people that I talk to speak of not being able to draw, or feeling inadequate as they try, or just feeling uncomfortable with the whole process of drawing. When asked when this realisation happened, it is often when someone has commented negatively in some way on their drawing or has requested help to understand what the drawing is meant to be interpreting. To develop Footnotes properly, I believe the individual needs to be released from the pressure of having to produce an image that has to be readable by anyone else. This is really important. When people are asked how to develop this inherent drawing ability rather than a learnt one, I encourage them to draw with a line continuously, without lifting the pencil

from the paper at any point. Once the person is comfortable with this, they should then begin to draw without looking at the drawing until it is complete, or at least make sure that they are looking at the object (or with closed eyes if drawing from the imagination) while drawing most of the drawing. In time, I encourage them to then use continuous drawing strategies, but to begin to look at the picture and reposition the pencil to start another stage in the drawing.

I was always the last one to be picked in any team activity, especially ball games, which I could not play well. My legs and arms just wouldn't do what I wanted them to. However, since drawing for at least a decade, I have found that my motor skills and co-ordination for ball games have developed very well, to the point that some people have commented that I am 'a natural' at them.

I believe that this is to do with hand-eye coordination developed through the activity of drawing without looking at my piece of paper, something that artists

are always encouraging their students to develop. In a sense, it cuts out the brain activity that has 'logical' control over the drawing action of the hand; if one was to see a table at an angle and only three legs were visible, there might be a temptation to draw four legs because logically we assume that a table will need four legs to stand. If the logical brain is constantly trying to 'correct' the message from the eye to the hand, this often complicates drawings.

It takes trust to draw without necessarily thinking about the subject from a logical point of view. The process of trusting the message from the eye to the hand develops an instinctive artistic response, which I believe can often be much stronger and more expressive than a response based on learnt knowledge or technique. This, therefore, is another reason why Footnotes strategies are so useful to many individuals whether they say they are good at drawing or not.

The grid

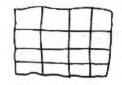

So far I have highlighted how difficulty sequencing is the main issue behind the struggles that dyslexics and visual thinkers have with words. I have suggested that communicating information in pictures is an effective way of relieving the pressure of having to find and sequence words. I now want to introduce the use of the Footnotes Grid as a tool for arranging and sequencing picture-based information.

The Footnotes Grid is simply a piece of A4 paper folded four or five times and then unfolded. The folds create a grid with 16 (or 32) equal blocks, and into these, pictures are drawn. The pictures do not need to be in a linear order – they can be anywhere in the grid. The idea is to create a sort of map of information, without worrying about the order it needs to go in. When you are able to see the whole thing down on paper, you can then decide how to link the various pictures to make a sequence. If necessary, the grid blocks can be ordered, either by numbering

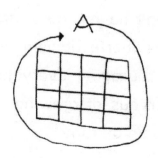

them or cutting them up and laying them out in sequence.

When drawing in the grid, the first picture that comes to mind is the one you put down. Don't think logically about it! Children are good at putting down an image that sounds like something but has nothing to do with the actual piece of information – as long as the image triggers the recall of information it doesn't matter what it is. Trust that the image will do the job – don't think about it too much. The pictures do not need to be high quality, so no inherent artistic skill is required; they will not need to mean anything to anyone else. The quicker you draw them, the better, because you can then move on to the next thought. Sometimes people who are good at drawing do not like using the grid when note-taking, for instance, because they don't have time to draw a 'good' picture. Try and put this perfectionism aside! The grid is great for encouraging everyone to draw, even those who are nervous of drawing, because quality is not an issue. It can be fun!

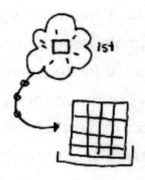

The next few pages give examples of ways you could use the grid, but before you get started, here are a few things to note...

→ The idea of putting information into regularly sized boxes encourages all the pictures to have equal value. Otherwise an oversized picture might appear dominant when you come to sequencing the information later on.

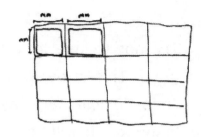

→ The grid is a template that can be adapted for many different uses, and often when it is given to a visual thinker a whole new way of using it emerges.

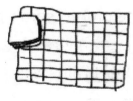

→ If you find thinking in pictures in this way uncomfortable, use that feeling to try and understand how a visual thinker feels when asked to think in words.

→ As an adult you may well feel that when using the grid for, say, note-taking, the information you are trying to take in is coming too fast to draw pictures. Try and fight that feeling, which is a result of having

used a linear, lexical way of processing for most of your life. Children generally find it much easier to activate the visual side of the brain, and have not yet developed a set way of processing.

→ Try not to use letters or words when filling in the grid. This is because if you suddenly switch to the linear-lexical pathway in the brain that deals with language, it will be much harder to jump back to the visual pathway you've just activated. It may be helpful to some people to add words to the grid, but it is important to only use key words because often the brain will focus on the words and therefore minimize the impact of the pictures.

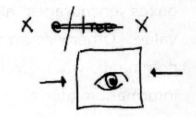

→ It may be that trying to do the grid will highlight an alternative preferred thinking style such as audio. If you have a dominant audio-memory, the grid will serve to act as a prompt to the audio memory.

There should be a sample grid inserted inside this book, and a smaller one on the back page. Why not use these grids to catch up on thoughts and ideas you've had while reading the book so far?

Note-taking grid.

Ideal for summarising information that is being given quickly, without having to write it down word for word, or trying to summarise in bullet points. Making notes in a lecture is a challenge even for people who can write fast. While you are processing what you are writing, the lecturer has moved on to the next point. Even with bullet points, if you return to them at a later date they often don't contain enough information for you to recall the full content. Perhaps you don't finish a sentence or you just can't read what you wrote! On the other hand, there is something experiential about drawing pictures - something personal. A picture can contain a whole package of information, and seeing what you have drawn can trigger the recall of that information very effectively.

Essay-planning grid.

The grid can act as a bridge between image-based information and linear, lexical information. Some dyslexics can write essays very well but it takes them a long time to plan them. Some of my students have found this frustrating, so I have helped them to plan essays in pictures, putting an idea/chapter in each grid square. The process of translation can then begin. One of my students regularly cut down his planning time from two weeks to three days using these techniques.

CASE STUDY: ALICE POVEY

Alice was not diagnosed as dyslexic until her first year at university. At primary school she had a low reading age and was weak at spelling, but extra reading lessons were the only extra support she received.

At secondary school she was given extra time to complete work, mainly because her poor spelling slowed her down. When she had to do a piece of writing, she recalls spending hours doing beautiful borders around the page and then even longer making each letter of each word look perfect. Her artistic creativity was channelled into every sentence, and if it wasn't good enough, her paper was screwed up and thrown away, and she started all over again. This perfectionism, although time consuming, was key to her success at school; her natural ability to be well organised and work very hard compensated for her weakness at reading and writing. Much to her credit, her strong artistic talent and hard work produced good grades. Behaviourally she did not disrupt the classroom environment, so her quiet and shy temperament together with her academic achievement resulted in her dyslexic tendencies going largely unnoticed.

Before going to university she worked as a waitress. In this busy, fast-paced environment her dyslexic tendencies began to show up more. She was given lots of things to do, and given them all at once, so when trying to recall and sequence everything she often got confused. She really struggled with the random, quick-fire instructions given to her in the restaurant environment and realised that she needed to visualise tasks ahead of time in order to avoid confusion.

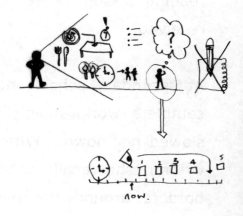

She came to University College Falmouth in 2004 and was diagnosed as dyslexic in her first year. University presented a new set of challenges for Alice, and more of her dyslexic tendencies surfaced.

She met Oliver, who introduced her to the Footnotes visual thinking techniques; the following are examples of the challenges that Alice faced in her degree and how Footnotes helped her to address them:

a. Assimilation of lots of new information through reading.

Alice was given a lot of reading to do, but had always found it difficult to make sense of written information. She usually found herself having to keep reading text over and over again to try and make it make sense, and often misunderstood it, putting her own meaning into it. She especially found reading in lines difficult, tending to jump between lines in a subconscious bid to understand the whole block of text in one go. Being a holistic, visual thinker, she needed to understand the context of the words she was reading, but needed to know that context before she could understand each word. Dyslexics like Alice struggle to process the words linearly, because

they want to understand the whole sentence/page/book at once.

Oliver encouraged Alice to summarise pieces of information in picture form on a Footnotes grid. As a visual thinker, Alice finds pictures a lot easier to comprehend, and was able to understand, annotate and recall the information presented in books much more easily. Oliver also encouraged Alice to use an additional strategy to accompany the Footnotes grid: she was advised to place a piece of tracing paper over a page of text and draw pictures on it, alongside the text as she read it. When she finished a page, she had a visual representation of that page, and understood this far better than the lexical representation.

b. Assimilation of lots of new information from lectures.

Alice found it difficult to follow what the speakers were saying in her lectures. Again, this was a sequencing issue as she struggled to create an image that enabled her to understand the linear string of words coming at her from the front. But she also found that certain things the lecturer said prompted her thoughts to run off at a tangent and she would lose track of where the lecture was going.

Alice began to use the Footnotes grid to take notes in pictures. Rather than try and scribble down every word the lecturer was saying, she listened to whole sentences or phrases and then summarised the ideas within those words in pictures. Not only was this a much faster and more efficient way of note-taking, it also created a far more useful set of notes for Alice to refer back to. She found that when she looked at pictures she had drawn a year or more

previously, she could instantly recall the information the picture represented.

In comparison, reading through written notes, if she ever did it, brought very little back.

c. Conceptual and critical thinking.

In school, Alice spent much time copying out blocks of text from textbooks; this was one of the ways that she learnt to assimilate information. However, her university course required her to engage in conceptual and critical thinking, which  was comparatively new to her. Having to think and reason for herself and come up with her own perspectives, opinions and arguments was hampered by the necessity to get her thoughts out of her head and onto paper. Words were an inadequate tool to process information and develop an argument – when she tried to write down her ideas she was distracted by trying to find the right words and then trying to write them correctly. In trying to write, she would lose her thoughts, and she found this very frustrating. In addition, the sheer time it took to try and write down her thoughts was in itself prohibitive.

So she began to use the Footnotes grid to brainstorm with. By thinking in pictures and then rapidly drawing those pictures in the grid, Alice was able to get her thoughts down on paper without fear of losing them while she tried to find the right words. Once she could see the pictures on paper, she was then able to translate them into words when necessary, without the pressure of processing at the same time.

d. Writing essays.

Once again, when faced with the challenge of writing an essay, Alice found structuring words and sentences into a linear progression very frustrating. Being a holistic thinker, she was prone to leaving words out, changing letters around, finishing a word with the beginning of the next word or putting the end of a sentence in the middle – all classic examples of the visual thinkers tendency to see the whole sentence in their heads but not be able to get it into words quickly enough. The sentences she was writing would usually make sense to her as she wrote, but when she came back to them later they did not make much sense. In other words her thoughts were flowing well, but writing didn't translate what was in her brain into sentences. She would end up writing and re-writing over and over again, trying to word correctly what she wanted to say.

When preparing to write an essay, she tried using the old-fashioned method of writing lots of notes and then trying to make those into an essay. But even when she did manage to write down her thoughts, she could not view the notes she had written in a holistic way. And if she had a break in between essay-writing attempts, she was totally lost on her return to her notes which were just a blur.

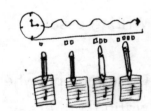

So she started using Footnotes as an organisational tool. She wrote the entire essay in pictures on the Footnotes grid, and then cut out each grid square and laid them all out on the table or floor. Looking at the whole essay, she then created an essay structure by moving the pictures around until she could see a linear progression of her thoughts. In this way she could visualise the whole essay – the pictures laid out in front of her made the essay three-dimensional and enabled her to see it unfolding visually. She often placed the pictures in a spiral, creating an essay that progressed from the centre outwards.

She would then begin the process of translation from pictures to words, free from the pressure of having to create an essay at the same time as writing it. Translation was done by talking about the pictures into a Dictaphone and then transcribing. Oliver advised Alice to monitor how many words each picture in her grid represented.

In this way she was able to meet the required word count for her essays.

Alice also believes that Footnotes rescued her from her natural tendency towards plagiarism; it is often difficult to state something better than the original writer, and the effort of trying to reword text can be soul destroying for dyslexics. Instead of just reading, making notes and summarising, Alice was thinking for herself and felt more intelligent and expressive. What she was writing was more 'her', and one of the amazing things about writing an essay in pictures is that nobody else can draw exactly the same image or have it contain the same meaning – Footnotes was the key to Alice's original thought, and enabled her to freely think around concepts and ideas and come up with her own perspectives and angles.

e. Giving presentations.

When asked to do verbal presentations, Alice found that she was getting overly concerned with the actual presentation of her material and this was hindering her ability to get her thoughts across. Like many dyslexics, she found it hard to explain clearly, using words, what she wanted to communicate. She was often concerned that people didn't understand her, and then found herself getting flustered as she tried too hard to explain what she meant and then felt like she was just waffling. She was frustrated that she couldn't easily say all that she wanted to express.

When younger, she used to use pictures to explain to people what she meant, so she took to the Footnotes techniques immediately. She began to use pictures in a Footnotes grid as prompts for her presentations rather than using notes in word form. Instead of struggling to read text as she presented, she could easily and quickly see what she wanted to say within her pictures. This not only boosted her confidence, it also ensured that by talking through one image at a time she said everything she wanted to say. It also helped reduce her stuttering and speeded up her speech.

f. Organisation

When it came to the last weeks of her degree, Alice had way too much to think about and do: designing business cards and a website for her new business, compiling her projects portfolio, arranging printing days and putting up her final degree show. With this pressure on top of her usual dyslexic issues, she was left utterly confused and didn't know what to do first or how to plan everything in order to get it all done in time. She luckily had a huge wall going spare in her room, and for everything she had to do, even the littlest thing, she drew a picture of it, cut it out and stuck it on the wall. She arranged the wall into a giant grid with large boxes divided by masking tape. The boxes contained projects in

the process of being done, projects that needed to be done and projects that she had finished. She could see in a visual table everything she had to do and she could physically move them around when she had finished them or when she wanted to work on one of them.

In summary, Alice finds that she understands pictures better than words. For her they are a more immediate and accurate translation of thoughts, and are a far more effective tool for communication than words, even though she was trained in words from an early age. She needs pictures to be able to visualise a concept, idea, essay or presentation as a whole, and has used Footnotes to process information, and to plan and develop her work. Visual thinking also made her degree work much more enjoyable – her essays and presentations became creative 'paintings' instead of chores.

Alice graduated from university in 2007. She is now self-employed as an illustrator, and is still developing and adapting her visual thinking techniques. After using Footnotes for some time now, she is now finding that she is remembering drawing the same images for particular words, so she has created her own picture dictionary. Drawn in an A6 booklet, the pages have alphabetical tags and each contains an image with a word or sentence underneath. She is learning to use her own unique language, and learning to trust that her images will communicate to her as faithfully as words can.

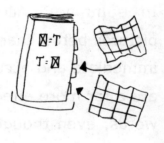

Visual thinking is particularly useful in her illustrative work, helping her to think conceptually and speeding up her processing. When doing an illustration, she would normally have had to draw from a written brief, but she now uses images to start off her illustrations – she looks at an image and starts describing it, using it to trigger off new ideas which birth even more Footnotes images. She ends up with lots and lots of images, from which she selects

the stronger ones; from those she brainstorms with more Footnotes, before finally narrowing down to a sketch of the final illustration. From there she chooses textures and colours before creating the finished product.

The Footnotes grid also enables her to view a project as a whole - she recently designed a line of themed greetings cards and used a 32 box grid, putting an image of each card in its own box so that she could view all the cards at once.

Alice says she still finds it difficult to be experimental with Footnotes, and wishes she had been told at an earlier age how to think in pictures as she still feels like a beginner. "I now think in my visual language most of the time, and I am aiming to use it 100% of the time. If it wasn't for Footnotes, I would probably find it very difficult to get my ideas into pictures. I'm really glad that I have been helped in this way – I wouldn't want to be 'normalised' and made like everyone else; I am more visual and I want to play to my strengths."

www.alicepovey.co.uk

Remembering grid

If you ask a child what they did at school today, they struggle to answer. The grid is used to annotate events during the day in picture form. This could be adapted into a form of journal or diary. The images they create are re-usable, so an icon vocabulary can be built up.

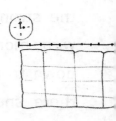

Learning grid

Similar to the above, but in more detail, annotating what has been learnt during the day. Pictures are used as memory triggers to recall new information learnt in lessons. This technique can be very useful for revision and exam/test preparation.

Distraction grid

This 32 box (5 fold) grid accompanies the learning grid – it is literally placed underneath it. For children who are easily distracted, this grid is used to hold their focus on the subject being taught. Any thoughts that come into the child's head that are not relevant to what is being taught, such as questions, emotions or unrelated ideas, need to be

dealt with swiftly in order to make progress. The child is therefore instructed to annotate these distracting thoughts on the distraction grid, with only 30 seconds allowed for each thought. They must then return to the main subject immediately. This strategy helps the child to let go of distracting thoughts, knowing that they can return to those thoughts later on and deal with them then.

Holistic thinkers can have several thoughts being processed at any one time, which can make it difficult to focus. If you are processing something and trying to write a sentence about it, and you suddenly wonder whether you left the oven on, you can't interrupt that sentence with this random thought "I wonder if I left the oven on?".

However, if you are making pictures from your thoughts, you can very easily and quickly squiggle an oven on the side of the paper and return to your original focus. Making images like this thereby allows you to offload your unrelated thoughts quickly onto paper while still retaining a focus. This helps to give a sense of control for holistic thinkers, allowing them to then focus on one thought, safe in the knowledge that the other thoughts will not be lost.

This strategy is useful for daydreamers in a classroom. Quite often a daydream is about something that needs to be done and the dreamer doesn't want to lose the experience he is caught up in, in case he forgets all about it. Drawing a quick picture of the daydream allows him to return to the focus of the class knowing that he can go back to the dream later using this trigger – it is not lost and is therefore easier to let go of. Some people might question whether it's a good idea to allow them to record a picture of something 'irrelevant', but the alternative is to lose them altogether or forbid them from thinking about anything else, which doesn't work if they are holistic thinkers. Trying to shut out the other thoughts is usually futile.

This strategy also gives the teacher a map of what the child has been thinking about during the day. It also allows the child to acknowledge what they have been thinking about, which they would otherwise not have noticed. A holistic thinker can be unaware of most of the thoughts and emotions that are going through their heads in a day.

Dyslexic learners often have a need to physically move around while they think. This can be quite disruptive and distracting in a classroom, so one of my strategies is to simulate this movement by drawing on a distraction grid what they *would* do if they were out of their chair.

Organisational grid

Most people find it difficult to hold onto a mental list of all the things they need to do. The organisational grid allows the person to quickly empty their heads of all their thoughts, in any order, by annotating each one in its own box. They can then be categorised in priority order, or sometimes cut up and put into a pile of 'prompt cards'. Again, this grid is useful for getting rid of distracting thoughts and allowing the mind to focus on one subject at a time.

Because of the issues with sequencing, dyslexics often have issues with personal management. A by-product of using images to process information is better short-term memory and concentration skills which can lead to better personal management; creating an image on paper or in the mind of something that needs to be done has proven to be an effective way of remembering it. This may mean that students have a little notebook that keeps coming out during the day; it will contain a visual map of their minds and what is going on in their lives.

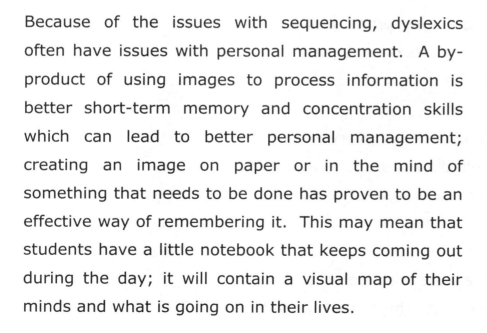

Spelling grid

This technique is designed not only to help children learn to spell, but also to take away the fear of words. It is a useful precursor to other spelling techniques such as synthetic phonics as it creates a space in their brains for processing letter-based information. It encourages children to enjoy spelling, getting them in the right frame of mind to learn new words and giving them confidence. Some may argue that synthetic phonics should always be the starting point for spelling, but I strongly believe that a visually dominant learner needs to establish *visual* letter/word processing as their primary skill; their audio cognition is not as dominant and should therefore be secondary.

This strategy has an element of discovery in it, and is therefore particularly suited to dyslexic learners who learn far better through facilitated discovery rather than linear instruction.

To start with, decide on a word that the child *wants* to spell, something personal to them that they'd be interested in learning how to spell. Because this is a visual learning strategy, it doesn't matter how long the word is. The child then draws a picture that represents that word to them, or an abstract image that they associate with the word. There does not have to be a 'logical' connection between the picture and the word – it is the process of imagining and creating the image that is important for imprinting on the brain. Drawing an image of something that just sounds like the word is often as good as something that directly describes it.

The word is then added (anywhere) to the picture in the child's own handwriting, with the teacher dictating the correct spelling at this stage. Again, it is important that the child uses their own 'font', no matter how untidy the writing, rather than being aided in shaping the letters correctly; this adds to the imprinting process. Remember that visual learners will learn the shape of a word rather than the rules for spelling it.

The next step is to ask the child to imagine their eyes are buckets, and that they need to look at the picture and fill up their eyes with it until they can close their eyes and still see the picture as clearly as if their eyes were open. When they are confident that they can see it clearly with their eyes shut, ask them while their eyes are still shut, "Can you see the picture?", and then, "Can you see the word in it?" and then, "How many letters are in it?" This last question helps them to recognise the scale and proportions of the word. If at any point they give a negative response, the process of filling the eyes is repeated.

When they are seeing the correct number of letters, they can then attempt to spell the word at the top of a piece of blank paper. Every time the word is spelt incorrectly, place a tick above those letters which are correct (and in the correct position within the word) and place a cross above those that aren't. Then fold over the piece of paper, concertina style, to hide that spelling attempt before repeating the process until the word is spelt correctly.

The grid can be filled up with various words, and then kept for future reference. It is important to keep a memory record of the words which have been spelt incorrectly; a visual learner will often have between five and ten possible ways of spelling a word and they will remember the incorrect spellings with the crosses above the wrong letters. This will in turn help them to remember the correct spelling at their next attempt to spell the word, as they recall the incorrect spellings alongside a picture of the correct spelling.

This may seem a laborious and time-consuming strategy, and teachers may argue that they wouldn't have the time to do it. However, the idea is that this strategy can soon be simulated in the mind within a few seconds. It is suggested as a short-term strategy, and the process should begin to happen in the mind within six weeks to six months. It must be noted that this is a strategy that the child can manage themselves after some initial instruction, and they are usually keen to do this as they enjoy it because it is drawing-based.

I believe that for some early years children with literacy difficulties, pictures in books can, ironically, be one of the biggest stumbling blocks to progress. If I were to design a set of early years books they would have no pictures in them – just space for pictures to be drawn. If the pictures are already there, the child has to try and store in their memory the word and the link to the picture. But if they themselves create a picture that reminds them of the word, the experience of having to think of a picture for the word, and drawing it, will enable them to learn it. I have seen this time and time again. Creating an image for a word is a completely different mental process than trying to link an existing picture with a word. For some visual thinking children, this is key to their progress in literacy.

I think the most important point for those helping individuals with their spellings is to remember that visual learners will learn the shape of a word rather than the rules for spelling it.

In view of the difference between a Visual and a Linear learner I do believe that this is a fundamental point and it is important that you trust the absolute importance of understanding that for a Visual Learner the word and image become one. Recall of this image in its entirety is what will enable the individual to find the appropriate letters in the appropriate order and indeed enhance their own ability to spell. For a Visual learner the drawing and word will make one image and not be segregated as an image plus a word in the way in which perhaps linear learners potentially store and recall information.

Sequential reading grid

This strategy is for facilitating reading of books of any length. First of all the teaching assistant copies out up to one hundred words of the book, five words on each line in the centre of an A4 page. (It is important to keep the words central on the page, as dyslexics are sensitive to the imbalanced shapes represented by the white space on either side of text). The child then draws a picture for every word on each line, in order, on the grid. The word is then added to the bottom of the picture, written in the child's own handwriting. The purpose of this exercise is to break up the words into manageable chunks, and remove the pictures that are present in the books. It is important that the images are created by the child, as visual thinkers need to use the creative part of their brains to make the pictures, rather than the photo-memory part of the brain that simply stores and recalls printed images.

When all one hundred words have been written out, they are read out first using the pictures, then using the words in the pictures, then the words on the A4

page, and then finally the book. Biff and Chip books (Oxford Reading Tree: Oxford University Press) work very well for this strategy.

CASE STUDY: JOHN

The following is a case study of a nine year old boy with a reading age of a five year old. John was the son of a farmer, and very practically involved in farm work from an early age, getting up at 6.30am to help milk the cows, driving tractors – generally very comfortable with the farm environment and confident responding to the requirements of farm life. When he went to school however, he felt totally inadequate. At the age of nine he barely knew his alphabet, let alone reading any words.

John's school contacted me once they had tried every scheme that was currently available, with limited success. They had primarily been using phonics-based learning strategies - the standard way of teaching children to read in many U.K. schools. They had heard about what I was doing, and invited me to come in and see John, along with others who were not improving at reading and spelling.

John was on reading Stage 1 of the Biff and Chip books, and had been for a long time. I sat with him, watched him read and noticed that he was completely reliant on the pictures in the book as a way of deducing what the words might mean. By nine years of age he was quite skilled at being able to predict what he was reading and was usually able to account for the story he had just read. But when it came to reading the words in another written context rather than in the book, the words meant nothing to him. When asked to read larger words and break down the words into sounds, he was unable to put the letter sounds together once he had sounded each letter out. In fact he still needed to be told what the sound of each letter was to start with. He seemed unable to remember the sound of a letter no matter how many times the phonics-based activity was used. He had apparently been on the same reading level for some years.

My first approach was to ask the ancillary to type out the words from the book onto two pages of A4 paper, ensuring that on most occasions there were no more than five words per line. The words were typed in a column down the centre of the paper as I felt John's short-term memory was one of the issues; a long sentence in one line would, I believe, be more easily forgotten than a sentence broken into two or more lines. I felt that the short lines enabled him to stay reading on the same line and be more coherent with his reading once he had attained an understanding of what the words were.

When I asked him to look at a large amount of writing (black text on white paper), John commented that the words were jumping about on the page. With some experimentation we found that he preferred to use light blue or light yellow plastic overlays, which seemed to dull down the shimmering effect of the words on his eyes.

Next I asked him to take each word that he couldn't read and draw a picture in a Footnotes grid of that word, writing the word in the neighbouring grid square if he knew how to spell it. This was important for him to be able to see his progress in learning how to 'translate' his pictures into words. Initially he was dealing with words such as Sam, up, in, cat and mat, all of which needed an image association to remember what they meant.

He also had to do a spelling for every word, and 'hide' the letters in the picture for that word. I then asked him where the letters were in the picture to reinforce the spelling process.

I got him to do a picture version of what he'd read, and then a spelt-out version of what he'd read, for the first two books. I went back two weeks later, and he was on his fourth book. His mother had come to the school delighted and his teacher was amazed that he was able to read with a confidence that he'd not had before. His skills continued to develop as a result of using visual thinking strategies on a regular basis. Instrumental in this was regular support from a teaching assistant who encouraged the use of the strategies.

As a by-product of his improved reading, over the next few weeks of the term his behaviour dramatically improved in the classroom; he was much more involved with the general classroom activities, answering questions as he'd never done before, and was confident to have an opinion of his own.

Reading comprehension grid

This strategy is similar to that of the sequential reading strategy, except that a whole sentence can be put into one picture. Once this stage is achieved, the individual can go on to develop images that hold more word content. This technique progresses so that the learner gradually creates images for greater and greater amounts of words, such as a series of images describing a whole chapter.

Speed reading grid

This strategy can be used by all ages as an aid to comprehending and summarising whole books; several of my undergraduate students use this strategy when working through a reading list in preparation for an essay. A chunk of text or even a whole chapter can be annotated in the grid to create a picture-based memory of its content. It is important not to worry about sequencing the information at this stage – the aim is to get an overall view of the relevant parts of a book. As each picture is drawn, it is given a page reference, and a corresponding bookmark with a picture on it is placed

in the book; in this way the information can be retrieved at a later stage and read in more depth. The bookmark can actually be created by tearing off a vertical strip of a grid, and putting an image in the top box for the chapter summary with further information about the chapter in the boxes below. A visual map is thereby created without copious notes, and the books with the most relevant content are easily and quickly identified.

One of my strategies for students who have long reading lists is to get them to spend a maximum of twenty minutes on each book. By skimming through a book they will get an idea of what that book has to offer them, and at the end they will be able to discard four to five books but still have two to three pages out of each of them that they wouldn't have otherwise had. The idea of holistically looking at a book is liberating for those who have only ever gone page by page in a linear way from start to finish. Those people feel they need to understand everything in the book and therefore have to read it from A through to Z, whereas someone like me who has never been able

to do A-Z has the confidence to pick up a book and look at G, K and C without it bothering them.

Instead of trying to reword their source material (which is usually well written in the first place!) I get students to make notes in pictures and then quantify how many words each picture represents. In this way they can break down the whole essay.

Big Picture Thinking grid

This is a technique for those who find it difficult to make sequential connection between ideas and thoughts or who suffer from short-term memory problems. It is particularly useful when faced with the pressure of having to make important choices or decisions, or when trying to plan for the future. Thoughts, options and ideas are drawn in the grid, and the picture making process, with its seemingly random images in no particular order, often proves to stimulate 'big picture' thinking, meaning that the person can see in one go how all the different components could (or already do) relate to each other. In my experience this has sometimes been

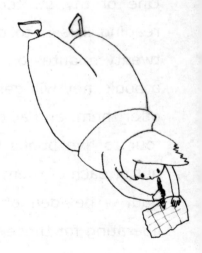

the first real opportunity that a visual thinker has had to recognise and recall different thoughts and ideas that often lead to a life-changing process of decision making. As well as being relevant for thinkers who have short-term memory issues and find it hard to sequence their thoughts, it is also useful for those who tend to overlook obvious ideas and thoughts because their minds are forever searching for deeper meaning (visual thinkers are often accused of over-complicating things). This enlightening experience is what can make it a profound and emotional exercise for visual thinkers.

CASE STUDY: SAM

A fourteen year old boy was frustrating staff because he was a bright and sometimes well-organised individual, but much of the time he really struggled with issues of concentration, memory recall and general presentation of knowledge learnt in school. Sam was spending a lot of time in isolation at school as a punishment, sometimes for days at a time. He had attendance problems, and when he did show up, he was barely participating in any learning. He was finally given an ultimatum: either he see Oliver or be expelled.

Oliver sat him down to do a Big Picture grid, asking him to draw what his life looked like at that time, what his future looked like and what he wanted to do with it. Through the process of talking through his images, Sam made connections between some of his aspirations and current interests and realised that he had a great interest in the fashion industry, moreover the design of textiles for the fashion industry. His grid also portrayed his life experience so far, including his family life and his father dying when he was young. All these perspectives combined for the first time to give him a possible focus for his future, which involved returning to his roots in Africa and establishing links between his family there and his business venture ideas in the U.K. With some help, he was able to take this a step further within a few weeks by obtaining a day's experience with textile students on a degree course. This helped him firm up the reality of his ideas. As a result, Sam became more focused in school, less prone to giving up at first sight of a challenge, and even his relating to others was no longer quite so negative – he had a positive edge that was not there before.

FURTHER INFORMATION…

I hope that this book has given you an introduction to my world! It is of course very difficult for me to put it into words and then condense these into a short book – I would much rather speak to you face-to-face. I am available for seminars, workshops, conferences and training sessions, so please do email me:

info@oliverwestfootnotes.com

and visit my websites for new book releases, Footnotes calendars and oliverwestfootnotes software:

www.oliverwest.net
www.oliverwestfootnotes.com

Thank you.

A MOTHER'S PERSPECTIVE

It is incredibly and intensely difficult to attempt to put on paper the battles and betrayals of Oli's school years. I find the anger is still raw, acute feelings of frustration and helplessness still raise pictures of my fists beating on closed doors. The memories of his daily dread of another day which he would 'fail', and later on the tremendous courage it took for him to board a plane and fly back to school to face another term alone still bring tears. My husband was posted abroad, and we sent Oli to boarding school in the U.K. because we thought we would be coming home soon and this school would better prepare him for the haul to 'O' Levels*. Only we didn't return and two years grew into five years, and by then the school had long ago said he would never pass an 'O' Level. I still weep at the pain of those years, but Oli says, "Yes Mum, but it was all for the best; if it wasn't so awful that I had to find a way through by myself, I couldn't be helping all these children now." True. By himself. Finding the way through.

I did have a session with one teacher at that school, taking him books and notes and references on dyslexia, and he said he was really interested and intended to find out more. "But I can't help Oliver, you understand – I don't teach him". They always said they were helping him all they could. Oli's judgement after 'O' Levels was that only one member of staff had actually helped him as opposed to just setting and correcting work; comments in his reports confirm this, and also their bafflement and inability to comprehend a pupil's way of thinking after five years in the classroom. Yet they said that if effort and hard work were counted he would have had straight 'A's all the way.

He would spend hours and days of his own time on his own on schoolwork, projects, revision – for English Lit. 'O' Level we bought Julius Caesar taped, and I read set books onto tape, and he learned them and got a handwritten 'C' grade – unbelievable! Looking back, he had listened and visualised until it was all in his long term memory, but he never read the books. From a letter I wrote to my mother: "Oliver wants to come to you and be quiet this weekend. I expect you will be helping him learn those Chemistry definitions. He needs to be quietly with you, he finds it so hard to keep concentration if he has to break off and resettle. When he is working at home he doesn't break off or stop until he has finished whatever. We just take messages and leave him alone." He got an 'A' second time around – I knew he somehow visualised or symbolised it all; what now also comes through is his ability or necessity to hyper-focus, excluding everything else until a particular objective has been completed. A second try 'B' for History has to have been long-term memory and pictures and symbols. Projects and essays would be bits of paper all over the floor, collected ideas,

78

notes and thoughts taken apart and reassembled. And then handwritten again. I remember the tremendous frustration, and the enormous concentration required to hold it all together in his mind, because it was all writing, it all had to be sequentially read and re-read and re-written. *There had to be a better way.*

Some of these tendencies, abilities, needs, complexities, were evident in Oli as a baby. Even as a small baby he would focus very hard, at other times be confused, very frustrated. By the time he was sitting, I was concerned enough to call the health visitor, because of 'different' responses to everyday things – total lack of interest in toys, baby stuff, books. A cuddly, lovely, happy baby sometimes, just not on the same wavelength. Hearing, sight, everything was tested – three times in about a year – all normal, apart from an obviously crazy mother who was probably causing anxiety in her baby. I now know from Oli's teaching that at times he would be hyper-focusing, and at other times bewildered by a volume or change of people and sounds and happenings, and either frustrated or frightened. That fits. As a toddler he was timid about new things until at about three we got a big climbing frame. Once above ground he just changed, became fearless, spatially 'at home' anywhere. He didn't do things the others did, not for long. He created, invented, was with the others yet doing his own thing. There always had to be more, bigger, and he could handle it all. Mighty frustration was in limitations he couldn't see the point of.

By about three, if I sang around the house, or a radio was droning on, (we didn't have TV) he would shout, "Be quiet, be quiet", and we still thought there might be some hearing sensitivity. He was an outdoor boy, and also drew and used paint a lot, as all small children do, using toys creatively, making big long term projects. Books were ignored but he listened to stories with concentration, and often while doing other things. Art was big and energy-charged, so they said he was hopeless at it, except for a local artist who said, "Heavens, they spend years at college learning to do that! He's a natural!" No one said that again until he left school. His confidence was by then so low, that even though he had enough grades for Art College entry he had to be coaxed all the way to his Foundation interview, expecting failure. They didn't laugh. And he hasn't stopped since. It wasn't about his belief in himself, it was about people recognising him, people trusting his judgement and abilities, other people recognising where he was.

But at every stage the constant was a big blanket lack of communication (even when Oli had been diagnosed as dyslexic – strange how once that label is on, expectation slots into zero), anguish over loss of self esteem and confidence, and sharp pity at real bullying and an underlying thread of mockery. We tried to help but knew that even we couldn't unlock the supposedly closed doors in his mind or find the end of the long, long ball of string which if unwound might become the nice straight line of sequential ideas teachers wanted.

There were battles, with teachers, with experts, with doctors over health concerns invariably put down to grades – why does everything come down to the primitive system of grades? I can still get very angry very quickly about our system, but through all the muddle, moves, homes, friends, and the ever present classroom in variations of familiar patterns Oli somehow noted, remembered, absorbed and found a way through for himself when it was needed. And there was a heap of school experience – Oliver knows schools, and knows teachers, and knows how children operate.

Because we are English and didn't know of any alternatives back then, we agonised over schooling in Oli's young life; in the English system you need qualifications to be employed and make a living. From an early age a child can be 'out of the running' for later and the struggle is excruciating for a caring parent, dealing with the daily battles and torments and agonising over how to best help, how to anticipate the years ahead. It is easier now. Apart from the slow dawning that people can 'get there' in different ways and different times, there are now other options. But the big problem is in the teachers' heads not the children's, that's the big one. I personally would now avoid the English system until Baccalaureate level because it is not ready or competent or adequate for my children. I would home tutor, getting computer literacy and getting the social contact in other creative ways. But most children are in schools, and we have to have people go in there and provide ways for children to find their own ways through the system.

My pain now is because of tough memories. Oli himself found his way through his problems, and is realising all his wonderful potential, and using it to help others. I can remember how it was to be told he would never pass an exam – better look out for some safe repetitive job for which he doesn't need literacy or numeracy. And for a while we heard it often enough not to hear anything else, and looked at the wrong colleges and training places for him, lots of them, because we couldn't find one that fit his gifts and character. Because no one but us recognised him. Until someone did. And that's what Oli does – he recognises people.

*'O' Levels were the first important exams taken by children aged 16 (GCSEs are the modern U.K. equivalent). The number obtained and the grades achieved determined whether the child went on to do two more years at school studying 'A' Levels, which are required to undertake a university degree in the U.K.

Elizabeth A. West

A PARENT'S PERSPECTIVE

"We have two sons who have completely different learning styles. Our eldest Adam was diagnosed as being ADHD and our youngest Clive is dyslexic and also has language disorder.

Adam has always found the restrictions of being forced to sit in a classroom for many hours each day difficult to handle especially when the lesson being taught isn't quite as exciting or challenging as a schoolboy could wish for. We have consulted three different psychologists and all recommended a variety of methods to help deal with the problem. None were realistic or helpful, especially the medication which had quite frightening consequences. Two years ago we consulted Oliver West but to be honest we didn't hold out much hope of him being able to help either. We couldn't have been more wrong. I remember sitting with Adam and Oliver whilst different strategies for helping to concentrate in the classroom were discussed. I must be honest I was a bit sceptical on hearing Oliver's recommendations but by this time I was willing to let Adam try anything. A few weeks later when I realized that the strategies were working I must admit to feeling very surprised. The teachers noticed a difference but were reluctant to admit to a difference in Adam's behaviour as he had been such a 'pain' in the classroom up until that point. I think they didn't want to tempt fate! Eventually it became clear that Adam had turned the corner and his reports have confirmed this belief. This in itself was amazing and we were thrilled by the results. However, I should add that perhaps the most critical issues to be addressed during the few brief sessions Adam had with Oliver were ones that Adam had been suffering with for most of his lifetime but was unable to talk about because he felt he would be ridiculed. He found talking to Oliver was so easy and because Oliver himself had suffered similar problems all Adams worries came tumbling out. Oliver was able to reassure Adam that all the thoughts and illusions he'd been experiencing were perfectly normal and nothing to worry about. In fact they should be welcomed as they showed that Adam had a wonderfully imaginative mind. It may not sound like a major breakthrough but to a mother who has seen her son suffering and being unable to help it was the most amazing act to witness.

Adam has made great strides since his few brief sessions with Oliver and now he is embarking on his International Baccalaureate with realistic expectations of passing to enable him to go to University. I never thought he would be in this position.

Our youngest son Clive is a totally different case altogether. Clive didn't speak clearly in sentences until he was about seven years old. He has always had extra English lessons and has been helped by speech therapists since he was three years old.

We discovered Oliver West shortly after we arrived in Geneva and arranged to meet with him. We found listening to Oliver fascinating and he was very open about his life as a dyslexic. It became obvious that Oliver had really suffered at school and in his early teens because of the lack of confidence that is quite often associated with dyslexics. Oliver has created strategies that have helped him to cope with school work and he is very keen to share them with others who have similar learning styles.

I think that for me and Clive the most important fact is that Oliver is a delightful person to be with and inspires all his students with his enthusiasm. Oliver is very down to earth and talks to all children/adults on the same level. Because he has experienced first hand how hard life for dyslexics can be, he can empathize with other dyslexics but he also shows them just how lucky they are to be visual thinkers and to have the benefits of being unlike others. I think that the most significant difference in Clive since his tutorials is his confidence. Not only is Clive able to converse openly with others, it can be hard to keep him quiet! Clive is also now looking ahead to further education and his main ambition is to make it to University. This in itself is pretty significant as before he didn't feel he was capable of gaining entry into any University.

Oliver's strategies are ones that work for people of all ages. I think introducing them at an early age can significantly assist children in not only their school work but also in their organization at home.

Both our children enjoyed every single minute of their time with Oliver and never for one moment felt as if the tutorials were a punishment for not succeeding or conforming to the 'norm' at school. We would have no hesitation in recommending Oliver West. Not only has he transformed the lives of my kids but has had a significant impact on ours too. Now that our children's development has been addressed effectively we are thoroughly enjoying their many successes and we look forward to, rather than dread, their last few years at school."

Use the grid below to help you record thoughts and ideas that you've had while reading this book…
